COVER PHOTO[2]

Cindy's Story

Cindy 1* was born by abortion at 27 weeks of development and left to die in the supply room of a large city hospital. No one knows who called the "blue code"- but forty minutes after her birth, Cindy was transferred to Children's Hospital. The trauma of premature birth has left her with cerebral palsy. She spent a long time in Children's Hospital before going to the first of a long series of foster homes.

At the age of five, Cindy was adopted. She was a very withdrawn child; silent and unresponsive. "They told us she could never be more than a 'vegetable,'" her adopting mother says. Cindy is now seven and is a different child. With loving parents, enthusiastic and affectionate brothers and sisters, and lots of cuddling, she is described by her mother and her teacher as a "ray of sunshine." No one in the household is more joyful and loving. She is learning to talk, and is learning more all the time because she is surrounded by family who delight in her.

Cindy has already saved a life. An adolescent friend of the family learned that a girl she knew was determined to abort her baby. She told her about Cindy, the happy child who was left to die. The idea of abortion was rejected and the baby lived to join the rest of us.

Cindy's parents have gone to court to get redress for the harm done to her. Since the case is still pending, details cannot be released; but they are hoping that financial provision can be obtained to support Cindy when she reaches adulthood.

---

[2]1* Where noted with an asterix, names and identifying details have been changed.

Introduction

Everyone is ambivalent about everything almost all the time. No less about life than other matters. Like every other species, humans depend upon an ecology whose balances, though robust and resistant to many kinds of assault, can become destructively and irrevocably tipped. The fact that humans, the self reflective animal, have such difficulty predicting and avoiding disaster has been a puzzle to philosophers and scientists for many generations.

There is little doubt that humans have both the propensity and the capability of destroying themselves. Their intelligence seems to blind them to the early indications that they are about to enter yet another holocaust of suffering and death. Is it because they have so much knowledge that they think they are wise? They ingest information in massive amounts, yet they have a great fear of finding any truth that implicates themselves as the real culprits rather than some remote, easily discernible villain. The best scapegoat is innocent and helpless. Hence millions of unborn children are made to suffer a painful death while in the assumed security of their mother's womb. Such pointless destruction is resulting in a huge disaster that is just beginning to become apparent.

Truth has never been popular. Maybe the more unpopular a fact or opinion the more truthful it is. The most unpopular or politically incorrect truth cannot be suppressed indefinitely. Eventually it will surface as a general outcry because, if for no other reason, it foreshadows or expresses suffering. Pain forces a complaint. Too often it is not spoken or heard until it is too late to cure the cancer from which it springs.

There are people who, by choice or chance, live when many others die. Yet, they do not appreciate or rejoice in their good fortune. This idea is not new but has always been disconcerting. Killing millions of voiceless and voteless unborn people ostensibly for good and therapeutic reasons is, if honestly faced, an even more disconcerting thought. Is it any wonder that combining two unpalatable realities, abortion and survivors, is not only unpopular, but is seen as subversive by most? When abortion survivors were first described[2] there were outbreaks of rage, but more frequently stony silence.

Listen everybody! We ignore the existence, plight and underlying problems of abortion survivors at our peril. We may kill unborn babies

---

[2]   Ney, PG. (1980) "A Consideration of Abortion Survivors," First World Congress of Victimology, Washington, DC.

and discard their bodies to avoid knowing the pain they experienced and represent, but their surviving siblings are present to remind us all of that most awful part of ourselves. Our tendency to scapegoat survivors is not easily ignored or explained away. Bit by bit they are driven by their pain and by growing awareness of the cause of that pain to speak their complaint. Though the world may not listen to our explanation of who, why and how they are, abortion survivors will be heard. But by then the underlying anger, ignorance, selfishness and dehumanisation will have caused so much destruction to human ecology it is unlikely the unbalances can be rectified.

AM I AN ABORTION SURVIVOR ?

Patient:

Doctor, I am desperate. I am depressed much of the time and often I think of killing myself. I cannot enjoy life.

I know that I have not used my abilities and opportunities well. I have always been that way, but now that I have lost my joy things are really bad. I keep wondering if people really like me and I am terrified they might reject me. I do not trust many people, particularly not my parents. Sometimes I have queer sensations of some little spirits bothering me. Frankly, I do not feel that I deserve to be alive. What is the matter with me? Am I going crazy?

Doctor:

Since my examination of you has ruled out most other probable causes for your distress, is it possible your mother had an abortion. If so, you would be a survivor. All your confused feelings, your doubts, fears and self-destructive tendencies could be explained by the fact that your mother aborted one of your siblings, or considered aborting you.

Patient:

You could be right. I have had these problems much of my life. I just found out my mother had an abortion. I have suspected it for a long time. I can remember as a child my father and mother whispering about her having become pregnant and what should they do? I was surprised when I did not get a little brother or sister, but I was too afraid to ask what happened. The topic of abortion came up in a discussion I overheard the other day. My mother informed her friend that she had an abortion but insisted it did not bother her. But I do not see why her abortion should trouble me; I strongly support a woman's right to choose.

Doctor:

People who have survived major disasters or deaths in the family or those who have survived death camps or starvation will often wonder why they should be alive when other people died. The effect seems to occur even if you are not fully aware of how you are a survivor.

Patient:

Well, I guess I am just lucky. I realise they could have aborted me. I was conceived shortly after my mother and father married, but I know they wanted me. Because they wanted me I am here today.

Doctor:

I wonder how you feel knowing that you are alive because you are wanted, while your brother or sister is dead because he or she was not wanted.

Patient:

It is a good feeling. It is wonderful to be wanted. But sometimes, even now, I wonder what would happen if I was not wanted? I wonder what would happen if people stopped liking me? I put an awful lot of effort into being popular. I guess it is because I need to be wanted. I am always looking over my shoulder to see how people react to what I do. I cannot be sure of the value of my own efforts without someone giving me an opinion.

Doctor:

You mentioned how insecure you feel and you wonder if you should be alive. That is a common feeling with people who have survived. They often feel they do not deserve to be alive; that the person who died was more deserving but died in their place. Abortion survivors wonder why fate or God selected them for life. They feel they now have to live a special kind of life to deserve their parents' choice to keep them alive.

Patient:

You are right. I feel this enormous burden that I have to be the best in everything that my parents could expect of a child, almost as if I had to compensate for something. Through most of my teenage years I tried very hard to please them. Eventually I gave up and became bitterly rebellious. It was not that they were so critical. It was this sense of being unworthy of all their love and attention. Now I see that it is possibly connected with knowing that my brother or sister died although he or she had done no wrong.

Doctor:

Many abortion survivors resent the fact that they are alive only because they were "wanted." It is such a tenuous thread by which to dangle a life.

Patient:

I have always wondered why I was so angry at my parents. They tried their best to make me feel wanted, but I now realise what a terrible dilemma that put me in. Obviously, if a child's first right is to be "wanted" then if they become unwanted they have no right to be. When my mother or father got mad, I felt it was because they did not want me. I remember thinking they might decide to get rid of me in some way. It is no wonder I thought about death so much. I wish that they could have said something like, "Whether we wanted you or not, you are welcome to the world." The other thing that really bothered me as a child was the feeling that I had to stay close to them. It is almost as if I could not believe they would still be there when I came back. Maybe it is because I was not sure if they would still want me. I guess I was not convinced of their love for me, even though they tried so hard to show it.

Doctor:

Abortion survivors have a type of anxious attachment to their parents. Part of that insecure attachment results from the child's worry about whether he or she is still "wanted." Part of it arises from the fact that many parents who have had abortions have difficulty bonding to subsequent children. Mothers who have aborted a child may also have more difficulty touching and breastfeeding subsequent children. The poor bonding exposes children to a greater chance of abuse or neglect. The anxious attachment tends to encourage children to be "clingy." Feeling that they must stick to their parents will inhibit a child's exploration which we now know is necessary for the proper development of their self-image and intelligence.

Patient:

Now that you mention it, I have always wondered why I could not finish my education or really go to the limits of my abilities. I am pretty passive about things. I always quit just when I am about to really succeed. I do not really believe I am good at anything. I feel guilty about not developing my potential. Attachment was a real problem when I was a teenager. I was part of a gang because I felt I could not count on them. I did not believe I was worthy of all the stuff my parents kept giving me. I suspected they were trying to prove they loved me when really they resented my existence. I got into drugs mainly because I did not like thinking about my life, whether I should be dead or alive. I did not really trust adults. It sure is hard not having somebody you can trust. I could never talk to my parents. I needed to ask lots of questions -- like, "How could you kill a helpless child" and "Why did you not abort me too?" Is this also connected with the fact that I am an aborition survivor?

Doctor:

You are beginning to make the associations. If you feel guilty about surviving you cannot fully participate in life. If you are worried about some event that could terminate your existence, you are not going to bother developing long term plans. You are more likely to live life "for the moment." Thus, in addition to your survivor guilt, you have an ontological guilt. You feel guilty about being alive and guilty about not developing your life.

Patient:

There are times when I feel as if I am living with a suspended death sentence. I feel I was supposed to die, not my brother or sister, and now some event will suddenly kill me. At times I felt so awful I wanted to die. Taking drugs did not help. I wanted to get high to escape reality. It seemed like any escape was better than what I was going through. I wonder if my parents discussed whether they would or would not abort me. It is awful to feel that they sat in judgement on an innocent child's life, especially since the child could not speak and defend himself. Someday I am going to ask them if they considered aborting me. There are some things I just have to know.

Doctor:

You talk as though you were partially aware of secrets about your mother's abortion and whether you would have been aborted. I suspect that these were not real secrets but pseudo-secrets, subjects you subconsciously agreed with them that you should not talk about -- probably because you did not want to upset them. After all, your survival depended on having parents.

Patient:

It is true. There were times when I wanted to find out more about my mother and about me, but I got the impression, I do not even know how, that certain issues would cause her great pain. She never was a particularly strong person. My father and she did not have a good marriage. Actually, she divorced my father a few years ago and now I do not go home much. I just did not want to make her depressed. Now I am wondering if she could talk about it. She might have been in better shape all those years.

Doctor:

When you cannot ask critical questions about life there are many matters about which your normal curiosity is inhibited. I suspect you also had to carefully guard what you said. You did not want to let slip something that would either make your mother sad, or frightened, or angry.

Patient:

When I was a child, there were many things that I wanted to know but I felt I should not ask my parents. It would have been so good to have their permission to ask or talk about anything. I am still careful about what I say. I hate to upset anyone. The free expression of my thoughts is so inhibited that sometimes I stammer.

Doctor:

I suspect being an abortion survivor had an effect on how you felt about your father.

Patient:

You got that right. I never liked my Dad. He was always such a wimp. He was never really there for me. He only thought about his job. He was no kind of role model. Besides, I did not trust him. How could you trust somebody who deserted your mother just when she needed him most, and as a consequence of that desertion she felt she had to abort my little brother? Now that I am talking about it more, I am quite sure that it was a brother — how I know I do not exactly know. As a child I often played with an imaginary brother.

8

Doctor:

It is not uncommon for abortion survivors to have imaginary siblings or playmates. Your difficulty in relating to your parents as a child may have carried over into your adult life. It would not surprise me if you have difficulty trusting men or women, especially about matters they would not openly discuss.

Patient:

I definitely do not trust women. I have had many girlfriends but something always seemed to go wrong. I guess I was looking for something that a woman could give me. Even though I am happily married right now, I still wonder if my wife might get pregnant and abort our baby without telling me. There are a lot of things we do not talk about. Maybe the same thing happened in her family. I know she did not have a good childhood. I wish I could really understand her. I do not trust men either. I cannot believe that they are able to support women in critical situations. I know that men do not have a legal right to stop an abortion, but I do not see why they will not at least try to intervene. I can also see why I do not have a high opinion of myself as a man.

Doctor:

Abortion survivors often try to protect their children from unforeseen dangers and become overprotective.

Patient:

It is true. I am undermining my children's confidence by always reminding them to be careful. I do not like them visiting their friends overnight or even going to summer camp.

Doctor:

If you would like your children to have a more open and secure childhood than you did, I suggest that the first thing you do is stop telling them that they were wanted. Emphasize the fact that they are welcome to the world just as they are, wanted or not.

Patient:

That is good advice, Doctor. Should I tell them that an uncle was killed by their grandmother? I suspect that they will never talk to her again.

Doctor:

That is a very difficult question. I think that you have learned from your childhood that you should not keep secrets to avoid being upset and upsetting others. There are very few real secrets in families. Most of them are pseudo-secrets. You now realise how damaging it is for a child to try and keep pseudo-secrets. Children should be informed as much as they need to be, *when* they need to be. You answer their questions when they ask them. Rather than giving them the whole story, you make it part of everyday conversation. I suspect that the first thing you need to do is to talk to your mother about this. She may be resistant to begin with, then angry, but if you are gently persistent I think that she will welcome the opportunity to talk about her abortion. The secret has been destructive to her as well as it has been to you. She will probably need some professional counselling. Your father should be involved also.

Patient:

Why is it so hard for me to know who I am, Doctor?

Doctor:

If you are guilty about existing and fear you might accidentally discover some terrible secret, you are not going to ask questions about the world or about yourself. If you do not ask questions about yourself, people will not give you corrective feedback. Since you are so determined to be "wanted," friends feel that they should tell you only good things about yourself. You suspect they are more often telling you what you want to hear rather than what you need to hear.

Patient:

I feel that I missed out on some very important parts of my childhood. Is there any chance that I can catch up on what I lost?

Doctor:

It is impossible to find most of the essential ingredients of childhood during your adult life. People do not want to nurture, guide, and protect you now in the way that you should have been when you were a child. Your wife and your friends do not want to be your parents. What you must do is mourn the loss of the childhood that you should have had and the person that you could have become. That is a lot harder than you think.

Patient:

Will I ever get over this? I am sick and tired of these self-destructive thoughts. I want to learn to love. I want to know who I am. I want to develop all my abilities.

Doctor:

You are already making a good start. There is more work to be done and you will not find it easy to resolve all these inner conflicts. I am glad that your wife is supportive. I hope that your friends and pastor also understand.

Patient:

I worry that what happened to me is affecting my family.

Doctor:

If it has this effect on you, of course it affects you family. You will need to talk to them as honestly as you can about being an abortion survivor. The more certain you are of your identity and meaning as a person, the better able your children are to model your good behaviour, consequently you will not have to spend so much time instructing and correcting them. Your wife can stop feeling guilty about not meeting the needs of your childhood. Once you have mourned the person you could have been, you will find that she is giving you more of what you really need than you saw before.

Patient:

I would like to put aside this burden of impossible expectations. In fact, I would like my parents to take them back. I cannot go on being sorry for being alive. If they are disappointed in me as a poor replacement for the child that they aborted it is not my fault. It is going to be difficult to forgive them until they apologise. I have tried many times to forgive, without success. Maybe I need to write down all the hurts and fears they caused and ask them to apologise for each one of them.

Doctor:

The process of reconciliation is complicated but forgiving, and being forgiven is essential to your health and welfare. I am sure you realise the importance of clear and honest communication with your parents. This is so hard when you cannot forgive each other.

Patient:

I wonder about all the millions of children like me who have had a brother or sister aborted, miscarried, stillborn, or die of accident. Is there a difference in how a person is affected by a pregnancy loss?

Doctor:

Children who die of stillbirths, miscarriages, accidents or even illness have been killed by events over which parents had little or no control. Children who are aborted are killed by the very people who ostensibly love their family. For this and many other reasons, abortion survivors have a much more difficult time dealing with the fact that they were chosen to live.

Patient:

There must be other kinds of abortion survivors.

Doctor:

Yes, there are ten types of abortion survivors. All of them have similar problems; guilt about being alive, fear of not being "wanted," difficulty with attachments, problems developing their potential, worries about the future, burdens of expectations that they cannot fulfil, trusting their parents, anger at authority and others. These are ten types of abortion survivors;

1. Children who had a statistically low chance of surviving a pregnancy. Children in some Eastern European countries have approximately a 20% chance of surviving through a pregnancy.

2. Children whose parents carefully considered terminating them *in utero*.

3. Children who have had a brother, or sister, or both aborted -- either before or after they were born.

4. Children who have been threatened by abortion. I have not infrequently heard, "You wretched, ungrateful child. I have sweated and saved for you but you do nothing with your life. I should have aborted you!"

5. Children who, because of their handicaps, or because they are the "wrong" sex, or because they are the result of a mixed marriage, would usually be aborted. Children with developmental defects often

wonder whether their parents would have aborted them if they had known about the handicaps.

6. Those children whose parents would have aborted them if they could have, being prevented only by lack of money, the law, etc.

7. Children whose parents could not make up their mind and delayed until it was too late.

8. Children whose twin was aborted. Twins have an intimate relationships in the womb. If one is aborted, the other feels a terrible loss and is often suicidal.

9. Children who survived an actual attempt to terminate their lives by saline, prostgladins or hysterotomy. They have difficult psychological struggles, nightmares, confused identities and a fear of doctors.

10.Those tiny children who survived an abortion for just a short period of time, only to be left to expire on a cold slab or to be smothered by abortion staff.

Patient:
That is terrible. Being an abortion survivor of one type or another must affect a large portion of young adults alive today. I wonder what it is doing to our world?

Doctor:
Since there are about 60 million abortions annually, there are at least that number of people who become abortion survivors each year. I suspect that it is the underlying reason for extensive family and social upheavals. Killing the defenseless has widespread ramifications and, unless it is stopped, it will result in some kind of holocaust. Aborting children destroys the delicate balances of human ecology.

Patient:
I hope that it is not too late for me to do something.

Doctor:
It is never too late to try. Whether you succeed in changing the world's attitude on abortion or not, you *can* change some lives. Most importantly, you will become more "human" yourself. After all, we are

all bound together in the bundle of life. We cannot benefit at the expense of our neighbour. When we love him or her we are loving ourselves and we discover that life is beautiful.

This drawing was done by an abortion survivor. It depicts him

receiving a lifeline through Christ out of a pit of despair.

SCIENTIFIC CONSIDERATIONS

Ten Types of Post-Abortion Survivor Syndrome

There is a strong resistance to the idea that people suffer when they know they could have been terminated. Yet, abortion survivors do exist. They will not go away just because it is difficult to think about them. Their distress and clinical illnesses should be recognised and treated. If this requires changing one's view about the world, maybe it is about time. After all, if these observations and deductions are correct, millions of people are badly conflicted and, often as a result, seriously ill.

In an earlier article[3] I (PGN) described abortion survivors and pointed out their conflicts are similar to those of people whose family members died in accidents, illnesses[4], or by genocide. Since that time, observations have brought to light the fact that there are at least ten types of survivors. Their situations and conflicts are different, but they have in common deep questions about whether they should be alive, whether they are worth anything to anybody, and whether they should develop their abilities. These people are not easily treated, but insight is valuable. It seems that when they sublimate their deepest anxieties into helping to prevent people from becoming abortion survivors they are functioning best.

The ten types of Post-Abortion Survivor Syndrome (PASS) are:

Statistical Survivors (PASS type 1)

These are people who survived in countries or cities where there is a statistically high probability that he/she would have been aborted. In most of North America, there is at least a 25% chance of being killed *in utero*. In some parts of eastern Europe there is a 80% chance that a survivor would have been terminated before he/she was born. If a person has a statistically slim chance of living through an event that kills many like him/her, he/she is truly a survivor and should be considered as such. Though many of these people were told they were definitely wanted, they know the odds were stacked against them. They wonder why they were allowed to live while others died. To be alive because you were wanted is not necessarily a pleasant experience or reassuring knowledge. It becomes quickly apparent to even children that if you live because you

---

[3]   Ney, PG. (1983). "A Consideration of Abortion Survivors, " *Child Psych Hum Development*, 13: 168-179.
[4]   Ney, PG. Barry, J.E. (1983). "Children Who Survive," *New Zealand Medical Journal*, 96:127-129.

were wanted, then when you become unwanted you may not be allowed to live. Agnes* stated:

> *Our country (Ukraine) is committing collective suicide. When I look at my family tree, I realise the number of people who are missing, missing in wars, sent to camps and who never came back, but most of all, all the children my own family killed. I would have had five brothers and sisters. My childhood would have been different. I would not have been so lonely. The state became my family, a big anonymous, protective family. It was a good system for me because I always needed to have people around me, otherwise I felt that I did not exist. However, my peers never replaced my brothers and sisters. I always had to compete with other children trying to be first and be well recognised by others. I guess that it just the way it was.*

Wanted Survivors (PASS type 2)

There are millions of children who have survived a serious deliberation by their parents or physicians about whether they were "wanted" and therefore should live or "unwanted" and be aborted. Their parents may have calculated whether there was enough money, the grandparents wondered if they could endure the embarrassment, and society may have questioned whether there were too many people in the world. The parents may have consulted a geneticist to determine whether the child was handicapped or the wrong sex, and if so had to make decisions whether the child should or should not be allowed to live. There is growing evidence that unborn children are affected by hormonal changes that result from major conflicts in the mind of the mother. There is also growing evidence that unborn infants not only hear, but remember conversations about them.[5] The implications are subtly conveyed to the child after he or she is born about whether he or she should have been allowed to live.[6]

◆[7] *"My parents always said they had wanted me. I often wonder what would have happened if they had not wanted me? I feel I must stay wanted. Being wanted means existing."*

---

[5] Chamberlain, D.B. (1992). "Is There Intelligence Before Birth?" *Pre-and Perinatal Psychology Journal,* 6(3): 217-237.

[6] Cavenar, J.O., Spaulding, J.G., Sullivan, J.L.l (1979). "Child's Reaction to Mother's Abortion, Case Report" *Military Med,* 144: 412-413.

[7] Quotations marked with a ◆ indicate actual responses from abortion

♦ *"I had fourteen years of psychotherapy because every year, as a child, I tried to commit suicide. I did not want to live. After many years of therapy, I found the cause of my distress. My mother had wanted to abort me but when she arrived at the abortion clinic, when she was on the table, she changed her mind. I do not know how I knew, but I knew there was something very wrong between my mother and I. Now I understand why I never wanted to live."*

Sibling Survivors (PASS type 3)

Many children are born into families where one or more of their siblings were aborted. Although parents believe it would be impossible for children to know about them, there are many clinical examples where children know that a brother or sister did not survive intrauterine life. One mother asked me (PGN) to interpret the dream of a very distraught girl, age 7. Her dream so disturbed her she was afraid to go to sleep. In the dream she had gone to a riverside to play with three young siblings. Together they had tunnelled into a sandbank, which had then collapsed, burying the three siblings. She alone escaped. She could not tell me the age, name or sex of these children. It turned out the mother had had three more pregnancies than she had live children, but insisted her daughter could never have known about these very early pregnancy losses. In one study of the impact on families of pregnancy termination for genetic reasons, it appears that "even very young children, and those sheltered from knowledge of the events, showed reaction to their parents' distress and maternal absence."[8]

Parents try hard to convince their surviving children that they were always wanted. Being wanted tends to make children struggle to continue being wanted. They try hard to keep pleasing their parents, and cling to them for security. But children must learn by experience. They must have a sufficiently confident attachment to their parents to not fear being away from them. Independently exploring the world is where children learn so much. Thus being a wanted child often interferes with intellectual development.

♦ *"I had no right to exist. I never grew up. I am still a child trying to find my place in this world. I have no goals. I am not attached to anything and never had a secure relationship. I was never a part of anything. I felt alone and threatened. My life, my existence were in question. I had insane explosions of anger and an uncontrollable rage. I*

survivors. They have only been edited to correct grammatical errors.

[8] Furlong, R.M., Black, R.B. (1984). "Pregnancy Termination for Genetic Indications: the Impact on Families" *Soc Work Health Care,* 10(1): 17-34.

was enraged at some vague thing that appeared life-threatening. It had to be life-threatening for me to feel such rage. I wanted babies, but when I had them I abandoned them. I went into drugs to escape this reality. It is only now, at the age of 55, that I am beginning to understand. A few years ago, just before dying, my mother told me that she had an abortion before I was born. Knowing about the conflicts of being an abortion survivor helps me understand, and it reassures me because now I know that I was not crazy."

Threatened Survivors (PASS type 4)

I have heard parents shout to their frustrating teenager, "You'll never know what I had to put up with having you, and you do not appreciate all my effort. I could have aborted you." Even if that parent never seriously considered aborting the child, that kind of outburst has a major effect on children, making them hateful toward their parents and destructive toward themselves. These children feel an awful obligation to their parents which they accept as a terrible burden or angrily reject. They cannot seem to enjoy life because they feel like they should not be alive. They do not develop their talents well, and are often seen as lazy, sometimes aggressive, and not infrequently antisocial children.

◆ *"I was fifteen when my mother, in a rage, told me she wished she would have aborted me. I was too much trouble. I left home shortly after that and lived with a man. We drank a lot and got into drugs. My life did not mean anything to me anymore. Two years later I had my first abortion."*

18

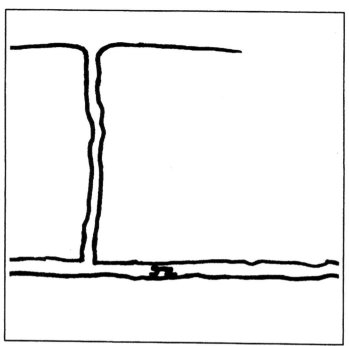

This drawing was done by a twenty-nine year old man whose mother aborted four siblings. He became a miner, then a psychologist. He wanted to go back into the womb and start again. This is the drawing of himself thin and tired, crawling toward a mine shaft for air and light.

Disabled Survivors (PASS type 5)

Modern diagnostic techniques make it possible for parents to choose only those unborn infants who appear not to have recognisable defects, or are the preferred sex. The knowledge that they might have been terminated fills the hearts of many developmentally delayed and handicapped children with dread. They know that many like them are being terminated, and that makes them feel vulnerable and ashamed. Even when a great deal of effort goes into giving these wounded people a sense of self worth, the efforts are undermined by the many implied messages in the media, that in the best interest of their parents or society they should not have been allowed to live.

Karen*, an intelligent woman in a wheelchair because of spina bifida stated:

> It is really hard having a handicap in today's world. Life
> is a struggle, every day is a struggle. Now when I hear

that they abort people who have the same handicap as I do, I feel fear, real deep fear. With euthanasia and all, I feel that my life is threatened. Now it is not only a struggle, I feel I am being persecuted. I have to be careful. I feel that people are starting to look at me differently. Almost as if they were asking: "Why is she alive? Did they not do prenatal testing in those days? I guess she was born before that." I am ashamed to be alive yet I love life. I wish I didn't have this feeling of overwhelming rejection."

Chance Survivors (PASS type 6)

There are children who would have been aborted if the mother had been able to obtain an abortion. These survivors are explicitly or implicitly told they were lucky to be alive because "if I had discovered I was pregnant earlier" or "if my parents had given permission" or "if someone had been willing or allowed to do it, I would have aborted you."

Sometimes circumstances arise that prevent a woman from having an abortion. Evidence shows that the largest number of women who are prevented from having an abortion are grateful once they see their beautiful child. There was no significant rise in the rate of maternal deaths due to "illegal" or "back street" abortions when funding for abortions was curtailed in the U.S.A. There are a few mothers who are resentful and convey this resentment to the child. "You are lucky to be alive." Unquestionably, children who are caught in this situation feel a great deal of ambivalence toward their parents. They may feel sympathy for parents about their dilemma and anger at themselves for being alive. Sometimes they reject and leave their parents. If they can find some other kind of parent, they may eventually gain a good impression of themselves. If there is no one to parent them, they quickly form an attachment to some type of leader or gang and thereby become delinquent.

◆ *"I heard my mother telling her friend that if abortion had been legal, she would have aborted me. It was a real shock to me. Now I do not believe her when she tells me she loves me."*

◆ *"I am alive by the skin of my teeth, or perhaps by the grace of God."*

Ambivalent Survivors (PASS type 7)

Children whose parents contemplated aborting them but could not make up their minds until it was too late to do an abortion are also a type

20

of survivor. Later in the child's life the mother is likely to indicate that "it would have been a lot easier and simpler if I had not had you." A child in these circumstances can easily conclude that his parents are still looking for an opportunity to terminate him or her. The delay in making up their minds is an expression of the universal ambivalence of people about new babies as they go through a crisis of incorporation.[9]

There is no doubt that almost every pregnancy creates a personal crisis. In the early stages most women are at least, for a period, unsure whether they want a child at this time. Often they debate whether they will or will not have the child, adopt out the child, or abort the infant. There are approximately fifty-five factors that a woman needs to consider carefully before she can make a rational decision. It is likely that most women eventually do not make a rational choice at all but are swayed by circumstances or emotions. Some women later convey to the child, "I could not make up my mind, but now I wish I had aborted you. Life would have been a lot easier and simpler." Some children who grow up under those circumstances are caught up in their parents' continuing ambivalence. Sometimes they are loved and other times they are hated. That ambivalence becomes part of the child's attitude toward him/herself and others.

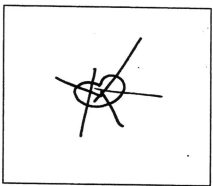

This spontaneous drawing was done by a three year old boy who was seen because he was "difficult." The embryo shaped representation of himself is in red, the sticks that stab this representation of himself are in black and purple. He is an abortion survivor.

---

[9]   Ney, P.G. & Peeters, M.A. "Deeply Damaged", *Pioneer Publishing*: Victoria, Canada, 1996.

Twin Survivors (PASS type 8)

Even when the most modern methods of locating and aborting a child are available, twins are sometimes missed by the abortionist. Those who have survived the abortion of their twin feel a great deal of anger and grief. One man, whose twin was aborted, becomes dangerously suicidal on the anniversary of that event. It is now known that twins communicate, touch, and even caress each other *in utero*. They have a very close intrauterine relationship,[10] and when parted grieve deeply. When one is killed, the other's grief is long and difficult. But when the grieving is for a twin you knew but never saw, it is almost impossible.

◆ *"My mother aborted my twin and then four months later she aborted me. I lived, but there is no sense in my living. I got into alcohol, drugs and child prostitution. I am not worth anything. Every year I try to commit suicide on the anniversary of my twin's death. I know that a death sentence was passed on me by my mother and that it still has to be carried out. That is why I always live on the edge. I cannot live and I cannot die. There is so much anger in me. I hate my father and I long for my mother."*

Attempted Murder Survivors (PASS type 9)

Gradually coming to light are a number of people who have survived an attempt to kill them *in utero*. Giana Jensen survived a saline abortion. She has some handicaps, but lives a full life. She overcomes much of her fear and resentment by speaking out for unborn children. At one point she had nightmares of abortionists trying to kill her. Ana-Rosa Rodriguez survived an attempt to abort her. She lost one arm in that attempt. One man, during his primal therapy, recovered a very early memory in which he felt extremely nauseated, suffocated and near death. He concluded it could only mean one thing. When he checked it out with his mother, she had indeed attempted to abort him. These survivors struggle with deep and difficult conflicts. "Why would my mother or father want to kill me?" "Am I supposed to be dead?" "Does she still want me to be dead?" "How can I trust myself?" "How can I trust her?"

Helen* survived an abortion many years ago with few physical effects, but has been plagued by psychiatric problems which require both medication and psychotherapy. She states,

> The knowledge I was a failed abortion makes me feel I
> have disobeyed and should not really be here; that I
> have no right to be a real person, and have no proper
> place in the world. I feel I was judged and sentenced,

---

[10]   Piontelli, A. (1989). "A Study on Twins Before and After Birth" *LtRev Psycho-Anal*, 16: 413-417.

but his punishment was not carried out and is still in abeyance. The hardest things to accept is that someone who professes to love me did try to kill me. For this same reason of broken trust, I have been unable to discuss this with my general practitioner. I have to overcome feelings of dread and panic when I visit him.

Murdered Survivors (PASS type 10)

Not infrequently, an infant that is aborted in the later months of pregnancy is born alive. Almost always, regardless of their viability, they are left to struggle alone and die on a counter or in a garbage can. Sometimes nurses are ordered to smother them with the placenta. It is the worst experience for any human to have to deliberately stifle the pitiable cries of a naked and helpless infant. Though these tiny survivors' lives are so short, they leave an indelible imprint on the minds of those who kill them. Neither time nor alcohol can erase the memory of having destroyed an innocent fellow human.

At the age of seventeen, a woman drew the picture of herself seen on the previous page. At the time, she did not know that her mother had tried to abort her. When her mother saw the drawing she screamed.

The child who is born after an abortion is, from a psychological point of view and for the parents, a replacement child. He or she carries the weight of parental expectations both for himself and the aborted child. He or she is often haunted by the presence of this "other" person. The "other" child, the aborted one might have been better, even a perfect child. A child born after an abortion usually arrives into the family while the mother is still grieving the loss of that "other" child. These children usually know that there is somebody "missing". Being alive because they were wanted, they believe they must always please others and therefore have difficulties being themselves.

Today more and more children are being brought into the abortion decision especially in the case of a eugenic abortion. They cannot remain neutral. The decision to abort a child because he or she is handicapped has terrible consequences on the surviving child. They are led to believe one is allowed to kill a person because he or she is not perfect. Their perception of any suffering persons will never be the same again, but they will experience relentless guilt that will plague them throughout their lives. They feel guilty because they feel they participated in the abortion decision, in fact or fantasy.

All children feel they have magical powers and can make things happen. In the abortion situation, their very existence precludes the existence of anybody else. ◆ *"Because I am alive, my sibling would not be allowed to live. I have decided that it would be better that my brother die because he would have been a burden."* Or they feel: ◆ *"Had I been a better child, less demanding, would my parents have aborted? Perhaps they dislike me so much, they do not want to have other children like me. I was a difficult birth and a difficult child."* This results in what we call the Cain Syndrome.

A sibling who believes he partook in killing an innocent human being, i.e. an aborted brother or sister, feels a double guilt. He was not punished. He suspects someone will discover what really happened, then everyone will know he is a murderer and want to kill him in revenge. He may now feel that he has an evil power within him. He may feel it is better to kill again rather then await a more terrible fate. Besides, the uncertainty is killing him. If he kills again at least the secret will be out that he is a killer and deserves to be punished.

Today there are children who kill in vicious murders, choosing victims who are readily accessible. How many of them partook at an early age in the decision to terminate a sibling? By murdering they try and resolve the deep conflict they felt by having been brought into the abortion decision. "I stood by helpless, ambivalent, unable to defend my brother." "I wanted to be the only child. I was glad they aborted it." "I thought it would be the best thing for my mother so I agreed. It was really bad for her and now I am guilty of two horrible harms." "I helped kill a baby and I agreed to something that harmed my mother. I am the one who should not be alive."

The psychological consequences of some abortion survivors are like those Cain suffered; being a wandering soul who must try and work hard (become an achiever) even though he knows that his efforts are not going to amount to much. He has a deep fear that somebody is "out to get him" and that he will be killed sooner or later. In our generation, for many people it is becoming safer either to kill yourself before somebody else does (a quick death by suicide or a slow death involving drugs, casual sex or smoking), or to be so strong that nobody will dare touch you. This tendency profoundly alters normal human relationships.

◆ ◆ ◆ ◆ ◆

Parents who have survived Nazi Death Camps have difficulty talking to their children. Often it seems easier to suppress the communication, but then the child's curiosity, fear and fantasies intensify. Professionals conclude it is better to deal with the subject of surviving directly. Parents who have dealt with their abortions find it is most useful to speak frankly with their children.[11] Initially there is often an outpouring of grief, many fears, some nightmares and psychosomatic complaints. In fact, children deal with the reality better than with innuendo and pseudo-secrets.

We hope that it is not trivialising to make the comparison with death camp survivors, but there are many basic similarities.[12] Helen* states that

> *Most disaster survivors are threatened by impersonal accidents of nature or, in the case of concentration camp survivors, by a hating adult enemy. Survivors of abortion attempts are threatened by those who profess to love them and it is this dichotomy of love and killing*

[11]   For further information see the companion booklet "How to Talk With Your Children About Your Abortion," also available through IIPLCARR.
[12]   Kestenberg, J. (1985). "Child Survivors of the Holocaust Forty Years Later: Reflections and Commentary" *J Am Acad Child Psychiatr*, 24:804-812.

that causes the unresolved problem. I was told by my psychotherapist that terminating a pregnancy is not the same as trying to kill someone, but speaking as and for the fetus, it does feel like it. I have the feeling that I disobeyed in not dying when it was required of me. The medical profession have been very kind although what I really want is for a doctor to put his arms around me and say that he is sorry and that I am worth something after all.

CONFLICTS AND SYMPTOMS

For the purposes of this booklet, a survivor is anyone who did not die when the chances of being killed were much higher than usual. There are many situations in which people become survivors, but abortion survivors are unique. The very parents who conceived them and who would normally love them have plotted to take their life or the life of their sibling. There can be no deeper enigma or more difficult psychological conflict. "My parents considered killing me" or "My parents killed my innocent little brother" or "My parents hired someone to kill me"... "How could they? What does it all mean? Why am I alive?"

People also become survivors when:
- some evil power tries to destroy their family tribe, race or religious group, e.g. Jews, Caribs, Newfoundland natives, etc.;
- there is a local or area wide disaster that wipes out large numbers of people nearby, e.g. volcanic eruption, famine, disease, plane crash, etc.;
- they are assaulted with an attempt to kill them;
- they survive some other type of possible pregnancy loss or their mother died in childbirth.

All of these groups have aspects of survivor guilt but they experience much less existential anxiety, anxious attachment, self-doubt, ontological guilt and secrecy than abortion survivors. In all of these other situations their parents almost invariably attempted to protect them against the force which threatened them all. The post-abortion survivor syndrome (like all syndromes) is a constellation of signs and symptoms, most of which appear in the majority of the people affected by a damaging agent.

It is generally accepted in medicine that the majority of distress and illness comes from conflict engendered disharmony of mind and body. Conflicts arise when humans cannot resolve competing or opposing

26

tendencies within themselves or when they cannot accept and deal with difficult realities or when there are major discrepancies between belief and behaviour. The following is a brief summary of the conflicts and symptoms that arise as a consequence of being an abortion survivor.

Survivor Guilt

"I should be grateful to be alive, but I should not have lived when others died. I experience guilt because I feel I contributed in some way to the decision to terminate them." People who feel this existential or survival guilt, because they were not aborted, believe that it is not fair that they are alive. They often feel they are not as worthy of life as those who died. People with these conflicts are always apologising for who they are or trying to justify themselves and their existence. They feel guilty about their needs and their dependency. When they become depressed they usually become suicidal. If they are anxious they tend to be almost hypomanic, desperately trying to please other people. Some feel haunted by the revengeful ghost of the aborted sibling.

◆ *"Why am I alive? It may be some outside circumstances, something I did or did not do. I do not deserve to be alive. I feel guilty. I am taking up somebody else's space, time. I wish I could regress to the moment it happened and analyse what happened. I want to fuse with my mother again."*

Existential Anxiety

"I want to live, but I fear I am doomed." People whose mothers have considered killing them or whose parents arranged for an abortion that failed, feel that they have escaped a death sentence. They believe that the death sentence is still in effect and may be carried out at any moment. They believe that because only "chance" kept them alive, "chance" will probably kill them. If they are alive because they are "wanted", they feel that they must stay wanted or they will no longer have the right to live. It is easy to make them feel ashamed. They are continually pleasing, fawning, "dancing," and hoping for applause. Eventually this becomes so tiring or time consuming that they become rebellious. The mindless vandalism of many adolescents seems to be an expression of their anger at being dangled by the tenuous thread of "wantedness." They quickly destroy or discard gifts given to them in an effort to remove any evidence of their parents' trying to buy their love. They tend to be fearful people who expect the worst. When they are no longer able to cope with normal defense mechanisms they engage in a variety of types of self injury. The pain or the blood is a reassurance that they are alive and not going crazy. It also seems to be a message, "Look, ye gods, I am trying to kill myself so you do not have to do it."

Because they are so uncertain about the future, abortion survivors have problems making real commitments although they readily make promises they know they will not be able to keep. ◆ *"I do not want others to change their minds about me. It is important to be well perceived by others. Therefore, I will make a commitment even if I know that I will not be able to keep it. A commitment is a real burden."*

They tend to procrastinate. ◆*"I cannot solve anything, so I procrastinate until eventually the other person breaks the commitment. I feel guilty about procrastinating, but I cannot stop myself."* ◆ *"I want to do what others want so I wait and see what they decide."* ◆ *"I prefer that somebody else decides for me. I had no right to exist. I am still a child trying to find a place in this world, like a little lamb, walking along side my mother trying to find a tit, a child wandering around, carrying the weight of something on my shoulders. I had so many unanswered questions which I could not ask because nobody would answer and besides which I could not even formulate them. All my life I have been running, running away from death, no from something worse than death."* ◆*"I suffered from a sense of impending doom which made me decide not to have children. Not having children made me suffer from biological guilt, because I knew I should have had children. I procrastinate then I feel guilty. I feel spiritual guilt. I am just caught up in a web of guilt. Everything in my life is guilt."*

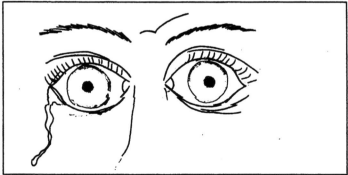

A thirty year old man whose mother aborted a sibling when he was seven years old drew this sad picture of himself as a child. It depicts him sorrowful and watchful; careful so that nothing bad could happen to him.

Anxious Attachment

"I want to be close to my parents, but it does not feel right. The closer I get the worse I feel." There is a well established connection between child abuse and abortion. A mother who has had abortions refused to hear the helpless cry of her unborn child. Subsequently, she has difficulty hearing her own helpless cry and those of others. She often responds with feelings of helplessness, anxiety or rage to the other children's cries. Clinical observations show that children born after an abortion often cry without any obvious cause for several months after their birth. Mothers testify that they have great difficulty in responding to their child's helpless cry. ♦*"My son was born two years after my abortion. He screamed day and night for two years. He needed constant body contact. No doctor knew what was wrong with him."* The anxious, ambivalent and tenuous attachment between parent and surviving child arises from three sources:

• Women who have had an abortion have difficulty in bonding to, touching and breastfeeding subsequent children. The mothers and fathers realise these basic difficulties and attempt to compensate with extra effort, doing it "by the book" and buying their child's love with gifts.

• The abortion surviving child is suspicious of parents and their expression of love. They think, "How could you, my father or mother, be a loving parent and..." "kill one of my siblings" or "consider killing me" or "have tried to kill me." "I do not trust you and I do not trust the anger that I feel toward you as a consequence. I must hide my anger or it will destroy us both."

• Abortion surviving infants often emit abnormal, anxious cries when their mother is out of sight. The toddlers cling persistently to the skirts of their mothers. One mother attested to the fact that her new-born child had screamed for two years without interruption and had needed continuous body contact during that period. This evokes in the mother very ambivalent feelings. She will try to push the child away, increasing his anxiety and his tendency to cling. Thus, a vicious cycle is initiated. Older children either are never at home or they hang around the house. Either way, this is detrimental to their development. Children need to feel confident to explore their environment and test their observations in order to develop their intellect.

As adults, abortion survivors with anxious attachment are continually asking each other, "Do you still love me?" They often say, ♦*"I needed other people around me otherwise I felt that I did not exist. I was afraid in any silence there was nobody around me."* ♦*"How could you, my parents, be loving to me and yet have killed one of my siblings or considered killing me or have tried to kill me? I must be on my guard.*

They might do something with me. I do not trust you and I do not trust the anger I feel towards you. I want to kill you. Yet I need you. It is safer if I can see and observe you all the time. I will do that until I am old enough to run away." ◆ *"I liked to be alone, my mother was dangerous. I had to be good. I could not upset my mother"*

Because they have no stable attachments, abortion survivors experience multiple fears: fears of death, of darkness, of a "boogy man" that will take them away, sometimes of fire or of knives. They think that the arbitrary event that took their sibling's life will eventually get to them too. As they live in fear of being terminated, they do not make plans for their future.

Anticipating the worst, they try desperately to remain in control of things. ◆ *"I often had terrible dreams, of great loaves of bread falling on me and engulfing me. When I told my mother she did not reassure me, she was even more frightened than I was. I did not understand why. My mother always told me that I was her favoured child, and I always thought to myself, "Why does she always have to insist that she loves me?"* ◆ *"My life stopped when I was ten. My mother came and woke me up one morning at six. She said, "Do you want a little sister? We would not have time for you anymore and we would not be able to go on holidays with you." I answered what she wanted to hear. I was half asleep, she was in a hurry, my father was in the car waiting to drive her to the hospital for her abortion. She left and my life stopped."* ◆ *"My mother was always distant, busy with a hundred things. She never hugged me. On the other hand, she was so anxious that I should get hurt. I never understood this distant but excessive control over me."*

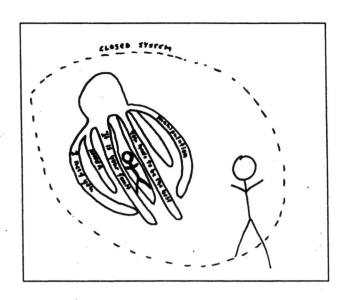

Drawing the childhood she had, a thirty-seven year old woman depicted herself trapped by her mother represented as a giant octopus. The family is contained within a closed system. Only father has one foot outside. On the enfolding arms of the octopus one can read *"anger,"* *"you have to be the best,"* *"manipulation,"* *"I need you,"* and *"It is all your fault."*

Pseudo-Secret Collusion

"I desperately need to know what you did to my unborn brother or sister, but I am afraid to ask." This conflict arises from two major sources;

• A child is afraid that what he or she will find out is too awful. In knowing the truth about his/her parents having killed his/her sibling or wanting to kill him/her, the child would despair. The child may refuse to eat, wondering whether he/she could ever know for sure that when they feed him/her they are not trying to poison him/her. ◆*"I was afraid of what I might discover. The worst thing would have been to discover that I was not loved even though they told me I was."*

• The abortion survivor knows that were he/she to bring up the forbidden subject it might destroy his/her parents or their relationship, and therefore the family upon which the child depends.

Children caught up in conflicts about secrets tend to be very careful about what they hear. They avoid the normal child's curious "eavesdropping." They are careful about what they see and avoid poking into family correspondence or archives. They are careful about what they say and will not ask things that normally tweak a child's interest. Their own anxiety and anger arising from a subconscious awareness of the pseudo-secret must be hidden. Therefore, they tend to repress all of their feelings. Children cut off the questioning of normal intellectual development. They must limit the expression of their speech and the expression of their emotions because they could be too dangerous. They become fearful children who do not express spontaneous joy and enthusiasm. As growing adolescents and adults, they tend to trust the media because they are confident it will lie to them and help support their and their parents' pseudo-secrets, e.g. "abortion does not kill a real child." They are very curious in spite of their determination not to know what really went on in their family. They have a voracious appetite for newspapers, magazines, novels, television, and almost any media that will provide them a certain amount of excitement but never reveal the real truth. The news creates a modicum of tense anticipation from expecting a disaster. They do not like to worry, but they feel worse when the tension stops. This vicious cycle is a major contribution to media addiction.

Distrust

"I want a committed relationship with people but I do not know who I can trust." Abortion survivors do not trust men because men, particularly their fathers, could have made a much greater effort to protect them from their mother's compelling interest in abortion. They may not trust men because many men have pressured women into abortions. Survivors later tend to look upon their fathers as "wimps" who were cowardly and could not provide a model for courage and tenacity in the face of destructive forces. It is obvious to the abortion survivors that males have a seldom mentioned selfish interest in having ready access to abortion. Survivors do not trust women because of their murderous or fearful selfishness. They cannot believe their expressions of affection are genuine. After all, they have killed a helpless sibling, often declaring "it is best for everyone." Survivors do not trust authority and cannot recognise leadership. Politicians and judges appear to cave into popular demands for abortion.

Abortion survivors become sceptical children who do not appreciate efforts made on their behalf and will not help around the house. As adults, they have great difficulty with committed relationships, but keep searching for someone that they can really trust. They experience a whole string of broken relationships, which only further convinces them they may as well be hedonistic. They tend to be narcissistic and cynical. Instead of seeing sex as sacred, they use it for self-gratification. ◆ *"I felt my mother was dangerous. I had to be good and not upset her. She had so many phobias, especially with knives. She was afraid of being left alone with old people or with babies. When I was nine years old she became pregnant and I was ill for nine months. I was so anxious I thought I was going mad. I could not eat anymore and was in a state of constant anxiety. I felt I was floating, I withdrew into an imaginary world of books. I felt like a dummy, not alive. I showed no interest in anything"* ◆ *"After her abortion, my mother slept with a butcher knife under her pillow. She scared me but I did not want to hurt her."* ◆ *"I always feared my grandmother and did not like to be around her. She seemed strange. It was only much later that I found out that she had had an abortion."* ◆ *"I had an acute panic attack in hospital one day when I was twelve. I had relapsed leukaemia and had had a bone marrow transplant. My mother told me she was going for prenatal diagnosis to make sure the baby was alright. I knew what would happen if the baby wasn't. One night I thought perhaps if I did not get better the doctors would get rid of me too. I never trusted my mother after that. In actual fact I never trusted anybody after that."* ◆ *"I never knew where I could turn for help, to whom could I talk? I didn't trust my parents, they aborted two of my siblings. Luckily I had a good girlfriend with whom I was able to talk."* ◆ *"During my psychoanalysis, I underwent a regression to the womb experience. I found myself on the floor, in fetal position, begging my mother to let me live. I promised her that I would be a good girl. I spent my entire life trying to justify my existence and being good to my mother. I still fear her, although she is 86. I never had any interest in anything except in books, because they allowed me to escape to an imaginary world."*

Self Doubt

"I want to live a spontaneous, natural, free and easy life, but whenever I try to, my impulses lead me into all sorts of trouble. I cannot trust myself and I cannot trust my parents. They obviously do not trust me because, having killed a helpless child, they do not trust themselves. They are continually hassling me about being careful and looking after myself, so how can I trust my emotions, desires or biological functions to guide me?" Abortion survivors tend to overeat, oversleep or drink in binges. In their most extreme form they are anorexic and bulimic. They tend to be "greenies" and/or hippies that turn into "yuppies" who compulsively watch their weight, diet and exercise. They aggressively defend their possessions and pleasures. ◆ *"I had so many fears during my childhood; fear of darkness, fear that something would destroy me, that somebody would take me away. I slept all covered up so that "thing" would not find me and destroy me. I think it is because my mother aborted my brother. I have so many aggressive feelings towards women. I long for fusion with my mother or with somebody, but I feared women. I want to hurt my girlfriends. I have difficulties making decisions. I am afraid of my past, afraid of what I might discover."*

Ontological Guilt

"I know I am talented and have lots of opportunities. I could have a good future, but I can't seem to get my act into gear." Survivors with the conflicts described here find it difficult to finish work projects, their education, or raising their family. They often feel that the future is too uncertain and they should not be alive anyhow. They keep quitting and starting again. Eventually they develop many rationalisations for their failures and become fully occupied with just living and entertaining themselves. They seem to be waiting for a major catastrophe that will propel them into doing something meaningful. They might subtly contribute to the promotion of a catastrophe, even those they ostensibly are trying to prevent. Unfulfilled, ontologically guilt-ridden parents often push their children into filling their own dreams that are usually inappropriate for the child's personality or intelligence. They are often good at rationalising their lack of effort. When asked to contribute in some way to a worthwhile endeavour, they are full of excuses. ◆ *"My existence depended on being wanted, but there is a lot of effort that I must put in to remaining wanted. I cannot be myself, I am vulnerable to all sorts of manipulations."* ◆ *"What do I do with my anger? What do I do with my fear? There is no reality, only my reality."* ◆ *"You cannot live, you cannot die. You cannot pass on that kind of life to others."* ◆ *"I had to look at other children to see how they behaved and I copied them."*

If a child cannot trust his or her parents, if he or she must always be on the lookout, then he or she does not feel free to explore the world. In addition, mothers who suffer from post-abortion syndrome are so afraid of losing their child they constantly tell the child to be careful. The anxiety is therefore reciprocal. Because these children are not free to explore and ask questions, the development of their intelligence is hampered. They become passive absorbers of information. Creativity, one of the greatest human gifts, is stifled. ◆ *"When I was four years old I suddenly decided that I did not want to play with dolls anymore. I wanted a real baby. One day I took my doll, painted male genitalia on it and then strangely enough I buried it at the end of the garden. It was only years later that I realised that my mother had had an abortion when I was four years old. Only now I see that to protect the image I had of my mother as being innocent I tried to make myself responsible for my mother's abortion. I have been carrying her guilt all my life and have suffered terribly from it."*

Dislike of Children

Abortion survivors tend to be unsure of their identity and existence. Therefore they are threatened by children. They avoid having children or committing themselves to family life. They will engage in any kind of sex that has little chance of propagating, e.g. "outercourse." If they have children, they tend to put them in day-care at a very early age. Many abortion survivors have a death wish which they know is incompatible with having their own children.

In addition to these major conflicts, most abortion survivors tend to have an undeveloped or poor self image. They may have perceptual abnormalities and be suspicious of being followed or spied upon. They tend to use chemical substances to deal with their deep conflicts. They try to avoid any real pursuit of truth and are easily swayed by the politically correct opinions. They inadvertently trouble women who are suffering from Post-Abortion Syndrome by contributing to the woman's painful awareness that she has destroyed something very precious, the survivor's equally loving sibling.

Most abortion survivors are sceptical. They feel that love does not exist and therefore they have difficulty reaching out to God in a trusting way. Because they have not experienced truly solid and trusting relationships within their family they avoid acknowledging people as parents and have difficulty seeing God as a loving Father. Abortion survivors may experience a deep sense of hopelessness.

So many parents have destroyed their young that there are fewer children in society, thus there is less anticipation for the future and less need to preserve for the children's sake. The lack of children produces hopelessness and the hopelessness undermines the desire to have children.

During the many encounters with children and adults born into families where there have been abortions, we realise that children intuitively "knew" that there was somebody else in the family, somebody that was missing. This is often expressed in dreams, imaginary siblings, who have names and with whom they play and or in feeling the presence of somebody who is constantly with them (a weight on their shoulders, somebody following them). One young women stated that she could not look in a mirror because she was afraid that she would see some other person. She could sense an "evil" presence and felt there was somebody missing. ♦"*I felt it was somebody very close to me, almost a twin brother or sister.*" Many children will spontaneously draw these missing children when they draw pictures of their families.

A woman reported telling her nine year old son about her abortion, which had taken place years before he was born. He said, ♦"*I knew, Mom, that there was something wrong. I always have nightmares about knives and my mother killing me. I have an imaginary brother who wants to kill me. If you had not aborted the other, would you have aborted me?*" Later in life he said once in anger, ♦"*You should have aborted me.*"

When she looked at the picture she had drawn of her childhood and "saw" the little brother she had always imagined she had, a thirty-five year old women suddenly understood that all the tragic history in her family was due to an abortion. She said, ♦"*As a child, I was too shut up in my own problems to even think I was an abortion survivor. I was just trying to survive and clean up the mess in my home.*"

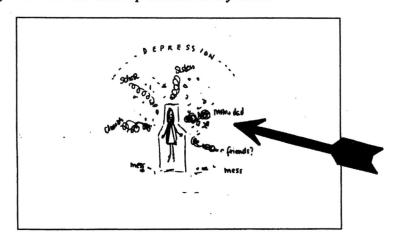

Drawing this picture of the childhood she had, she put herself in a box (or coffin) surrounded by chaos, fighting and confusion.

Suddenly she realised that she had drawn a little stick figure under her parents, outside a little box (womb?). At that moment it dawned on her that she was an abortion survivor and that all the pain in her childhood could be traced to the abortion event.

HOW COULD A CHILD KNOW?

They guess

Because abortion is often discussed at school and in the media, children wonder whether there might not have been an abortion in their own family. Thinking about their parents' circumstances and knowing their parents' personality, they guess that a sibling may have been aborted. They wonder whether their parents may have considered aborting *them*. Once they are suspicious, they look for corroborating evidence.

By intuition

By means that are hard to describe, children sense they have a sibling that is not present. This intuitive knowledge shows up in dreams or as imaginary playmates, or in illusions, e.g. a brief glimpse of a small child hiding behind a tree. Children, when asked to draw a picture of everybody in their family, may draw in an extra child or two. Parents may be confronted with innocent questions. "Mummy, I always thought there was another baby in our family. Is there somebody missing?"

They question pseudo-secrets

Children are usually aware that there are certain family subjects they should not talk about. Gaps in their knowledge of the family indicate what that subject may be, and they become very curious. They dare not ask because they fear retribution to themselves or upset to their family. Not infrequently the gap or pseudo secret preys on their mind until they just have to find out.

They indirectly probe

Children, when curious about relationships, often ask their parents indirectly about "family secrets." By their parents' evasive answers they suspect that the real answer is true to their worst fears. "Mummy, how old were you when I was born?" "When you went to the clinic, did they find anything wrong? You didn't look so good when you came home."

They overhear

Children may hear their parents talk about an abortion when they are supposed to be asleep or away playing. They may overhear a telephone conversation or friends or grandparents worrying out loud. The conversation may be indistinct, but there is usually sufficient information to let their children guess that the real content is about an abortion in the family.

Little spirits seem to speak

. Some people believe that children are made aware of the existence of an aborted sibling by the presence of a little spirit who might bother them in the night or when they are alone. Young children are usually more curious than frightened, but by their parents' reaction they know it is not something to talk about.

They are asked to participate in a decision about aborting the next pregnancy

Although this sounds appalling, some parents feel it is the right and democratic way to involve their children in a discussion about whether the present pregnancy should be aborted. The child will guess that this may already have happened to a sibling or could have happened to them.

They deduce from family difficulties

Because abortion is becoming topical, intelligent children soon begin to wonder if the difficulties their parents are experiencing do not stem from an abortion. Learning about the Post-Abortion Syndrome makes it possible for young people to realise that the guilt and oppression their parents are experiencing for no apparent reason are probably a consequence of an abortion.

Parents blurt it out

Sometimes parents, in exasperation with a recalcitrant, rebellious child, will shout, "You ungrateful little wretch. I have spent my life looking after you. Don't you realise that I could have (or should have) aborted you?"

Children are told directly

Some parents will tell their child directly because they believe in open family communication. Unhappily, these children are given little chance to ask questions or discuss their strong mixed feelings.

CLINICAL CASES

Michelle

Michelle* is an intelligent four year old girl, abandoned at birth and adopted at two years of age.

One day she gave her adoptive mother a drawing together with the following explanations: *"This is a mommy. She has a baby in her tummy. He is covered with blood. The mommy is bad. She kicks the baby and hits him and spits on him. But the baby is a good baby."* She then began hitting the picture of the mother and shouting: *"She is bad, she is bad."* Her mother asked her: *"And the baby - do you hit him, too?"* Michelle responded, *"No, the baby is a good baby."* She protected the baby by covering him with her hand. Her mother told her that she liked her drawings and wants to have some more.

Michelle did not know that she had been conceived during a rape and that her real mother had tried to abort her (using knitting needles). Her parents found this out when they adopted Michelle, but the child was never told. Michelle only knew that she had been adopted.

A few days after drawing the first picture, Michelle showed her mother a similar drawing. This time, however, there was a black object close to the baby's head. It was bent and the child explained that it was a hook.

Eight days later she drew the same type of picture a third time. Her adoptive mother asked her: *"Do you think the baby can forgive his mother for hurting him?"* immediately the child answered: *"No, because she killed ME."* It was the first time Michelle had used the first person in talking about the baby.

39

This drawing was done by Michelle. It depicts her mother. The "baby" in the mother's abdomen (womb) is drawn in red.

Kathy

I have a husband and three children. I am employed as a pastoral counsellor with my church. In my early twenties I became pregnant with my son out of marriage. At the time, I was living in South America, where abortion is still illegal. My boyfriend and his parents put a lot of pressure on me to have an abortion. I was appalled by their attitudes. Although I was a lapsed churchgoer, I knew in my heart that abortion is murder.

I was very hurt to think that the father of my baby wanted me to get rid of it in such a cruel way. It could be that my PASS symptoms made me identify more strongly with the baby and helped to intensify the fiercely protective feelings I had towards it.

I believe that God helped me to stick to my decision because I am not naturally morally courageous. I have always been extremely grateful that I did. Today I have a twenty-one year old son who is currently completing a physics degree at university. He is also a young man of God. The world would be a much poorer place without him and so would my life and the lives of many others, including his father.

Though successful at most things I do, I have a sense of inner abandonment and desolation. I am always vainly searching for a home. I am always hungry with an insatiable hunger for love. I always need reassurance to justify my existence by doing it right and being good. At times I have a deep, murderous hatred of children. This baffles me. I do not want to hate children, and I really feel for unwanted kids.

Before receiving help I had no joy and no awareness of nature. I experienced frequent physical sensations of dipping and swaying and balance changes like a baby in the womb. Visual images which haunt my mind are of a ghostly figure suspended between earth and heaven, fleeing over the rooftops of a war devastated city. My mother aborted in the city of London during the war with bombs and dust and with buildings going up in flames. My strange sensation of being suspended over a bombed city does not come from any stories I have heard or any pictures I have seen. Only my mother would have known about it. She and her aborted baby.

I knew I had to go on the Hope Alive group therapy training conference although I did not know why. Even at such short notice I was inexplicably able to make the time free! As soon as we began the round that Sunday evening, I knew I would have to speak about my mother's abortion. I had no idea then of the Post-Abortion Survivor Syndrome (PASS). Even now as I write I have deliberately avoided reading anything about it.

At the training session, after I described this phenomenon, the trainer suggested that this was typical of PASS. It was a great relief to know that at last someone understood what I had been trying to explain for years. Suddenly, something I had only dimly been able to grasp through the ephemeral language of dreams now had a name. There was also an explanation for the strange physical sensations I sometimes experienced, the somatic memories of pregnancy, feelings of dipping and swaying, with an accompanying fogginess of mind. To have someone hear me, believe me and understand me for the first time in my life was like recognising that little girl in the shadow with her dark secret for the first time ever.

I once had an unusual experience where I relived my mother aborting my sister. I felt an overwhelming feeling of wanting to die. I felt terrible abdominal pain, skin prickling, pain in the umbilical area and a sense of black poison pouring into me. This poison was an intense hatred of children. I went through some time of screaming the terrible screams that have always lurked below the surface and often threatened to come out. At last, I found myself in a safe enough place to express them. I am very grateful that I was believed and taken seriously.

Since last year I have searched my mind for the explanation for the knowledge I received non-verbally from my mother. She died when I was twenty-one and never told me about her abortion. My father

41

mentioned it very briefly in passing during a conversation about my mother when I was twenty-five. He offered it as a possible explanation for her irascible temper, but we did not discuss it any further. Immediately I felt that it had to be a key, but have only recently come to realise more fully its impact on both her and me.

It must be borne in mind that the secret knowledge I received regarding my mother's abortion was accurate and detailed enough to specifically influence my perceptions of myself, my mother and, to some extent, the safety of the world I was born into. I believe that this information was transmitted to me in the womb with sufficient sophistication of perception to determine some of my deepest beliefs about life. My own identity and personality has been overlaid and haunted by both the presence and the experience of the aborted baby. I feel as if I have lived my whole life under the control of the spirit and the experience of the dead child. At certain times this impression has been made more intense by threatening or painful experiences. My mother's abortion, perpetrated years before I was born and the child of a different father, has had the most profound influence on my life.

It is not possible to give more than a speculative explanation as to how I came by the secret knowledge of my mother's abortion. The knowledge could have been transmitted "transitionally" through some spiritual or psychic connection. Some would explain that it came through the "unquiet spirit" of the dead child. Others, that it was the work of a demonic "familiar" or "guiding" spirit impersonating the aborted child. For the Jungian, it might be understood to be the result of a collective consciousness. I am not sure of the explanations, but I am convinced about my own feelings.

I have the feeling that I do not have the right to live and therefore no right to the good things of life, no right to possess things, no right to an education. I have no sense of belonging to the world or life. Relationships always have to be worked out through the servile role of the little black servant girl, the Cinderella figure. At other times, I play the superior role with those I consider to be inferior to me.

There is the wounded, bewildered, lost person who does not know where she belongs. She is rootless, wandering stateless, landless, looking and searching for home. She is a lonely, haunted, longing little girl, always on the outside, pressing her nose against the window of life, wanting to get in. She senses that there are many lost presences out there longing to be allowed in; the world's orphans, longing to be allowed into the family of man. They are rejected and locked out, longing, alone, lost, lonely, haunted and dark. They are unseen, unknown, *unacknowledged,*

42

unclaimed, unnamed and lost to life. Their haunting presence is always around.

The little servant girl is guilty of living. She does not deserve to live. She has no place on stage, no central place in life, to role to play. No one wants her; no one wants to hear her lines. They are too sad and dark, painful and challenging. Her eyes speak too much truth. She has seen too much. There is a conspiracy to keep her hidden in the dark. She is the silent repository of the world's shame, the world's guilt and pain. And she had better suffer silently so they can go on laughing on the bright side of their faces.

No one wants to face her reality. She judges the world by her innocent pain, her broken exposure, her shameful wounds. She has got too much to say in silent innocence, the eloquence of her wide gaze shames the creatures of the night. So I hid her too for shame and hid with her in the shadows.

It is like an angry parent finding the naughty child hiding behind the couch and dragging him out, unwilling, ashamed, helpless, angry, alone, friendless, no ally to help. The parent is right, of course. Might is right, and the child is wrong, helplessly to blame, shamefully existent, shamefully alive. It is not my wounds which pain me the most, nor even my shameful bruises. It is not being heard. It is being sentenced to silence that hurts the most. Worse than not being seen is not being heard.

That is who I have always been really, someone waiting to be really seen and, hope beyond all glorious hope, waiting to be heard. I was someone waiting to happen. I often struggle with weariness and a feeling of heaviness as if it is a struggle to stay alive. I seem to be constantly fighting off death which feels immanent and deeply desired. I long to be able to stoop with struggle of life -- the struggle to stay alive, preferring to be allowed to lie down and die. I want to quietly slide into oblivion and give up the fight. I seem to be living under the sentence of death all the time.

When you have seen death with your inner eyes, tasted the blood in your mouth, felt the mushy flesh in your hands, you can never pretend life out there is any more then a pretence. The inner reality is too terrible, too real, too immediate to ever give yourself to anything else. This surrogate pregnancy grips your inner attention so only the outer smile of you enters life. Your inner self is bearing death -- the wounds and static blood of death.

You are bound to carry that death thing forever. No birth can release you. The birth of your own children involves only the outer shell of you as does all you interaction out there. It is easy to give all that away. It really does not count anyway. The real person is carrying death within, a dark secret hidden under the covers of silence, known only to the deepest heart of a girl who has drawn life (or death) from the depth of her mother's being, known only to the two of them. The girl has lain close to her mother's heart and drunk deep of her death and learnt from the womb to reject her.

Only the errant temper leaked out around the edges of my self-control. That temper took control over me sometimes. I read murder and hatred in my mother's eyes and lived under her judgement of death. I was punished for my weakness, my vulnerability, my need and daring to be all those things. I dared to impose my need on her, to depend on her, challenge her selfishness, asking her for her sustenance, support and care.

My mother gave me just enough to stay alive, but not enough to live. She carefully maintained a precarious balance between appeasing guilt and keeping her heart under wraps. So I was allowed to stay alive but not to live. In the meantime, she subjected me to the same treatment of her inner heart. I was allowed to be alive but not to live. She denied me as much life as was decently possible without actually killing me.

When I began to tell my story and the others in the training group listened, I could not hold my hurt and terror back any longer. Suddenly I could feel the awful screams which had been locked up inside me coming out. As all the pain started unlocking, I felt myself sliding off my chair onto the floor. I felt very vulnerable and fetal, strangely unable to move or escape my inevitable fate. My skin was burning and I kept plucking at it, trying to escape the pain. I could feel black, poisonous hatred pouring into me through my umbilical cord. All the collective hatred against children through the generations poured into me and I knew it would kill me.

The pain in my stomach was terrible and closely associated with the black poison pouring into me through the umbilical cord. I can only assume that this was the emotional hatred and murder my mother felt towards the unborn child, my older sister. I could feel the fetal attempts to escape and the feeble efforts to move the head out of the way. I do not know how that baby died, but from what I experienced that night, I imagine it was a saline injection or something similar. I do not know how old it was either, but it was aware enough to know it was in mortal danger and that it had to try its best to escape.

A lot more happened during that week of training, but defusing the abortion memory was the most significant for me. Since then, the somatic memories still occasionally recur. I do not experience abdominal pain or the same measure of panic and fluttering. I have prayed about the fear of death, a death wish, guilt and the feelings of living under the shadow of death because of my mother's judgements on me and her other daughter. I do not feel so panicked about authority either. Best of all, I do not live through my sister, Monica, any more.

So, I connected me with me for the first time ever. It gave me permission to actually give that little dark girl the opportunity to be heard, to take centre stage, to retire Monica and be seen and heard for the first time in a friendly, accepting, wise and knowing environment.

During my Christian life, God has given me many revelations and healed me in many areas, but none more profound than the healing I have received from the influences of my PASS experience. I know that Jesus Christ of Nazareth suffered the sentence of death for me in order that I might be reconciled to the Father. I no longer live under the judgement of death, but in the light of His love, in the kingdom of the Son of His love. For that, I will be forever grateful.

Author's Note:
Though her story may seem implausible and "crazy" to some, it is true. Kathy is a well respected, active Christian counsellor. She has come to realize the intense and deep effect that being an abortion survivor has had on her life, and has taken steps to knowing and growing from her experience.

Jean Paul

I am a forty-nine year old street worker in a large American centre. I am concerned mostly with the poor and immigrants. About thirty years ago I found out that my mother was actually my stepmother and I began to investigate about my dad's prior marriage. It turned out that in the mid 1940's he was married to my birth mother. Eventually I was able to track her down and she told me about the disastrous relationship she had with my dad. It was a marriage mostly of convenience. My father was an officer in the armed forces and had a premonition that he would not "make it back." He desperately wanted a child to survive him so he pressured my mother into having sex without contraception. When she found that she was pregnant she was so angry that she arranged for an abortion in her fourth month.

That abortion was only 50% successful. She terminated my twin brother. At seven months she recognised she was still pregnant and went for a second abortion. This time it was me. I was three and a half pound, epileptic, jaundiced and dying. A good-hearted woman at the brothel where the abortion took place decided to try and save me. After a time in the hospital and then the brothel, I was placed in a foundling home. Quite by accident (some six months later) my father discovered me. I was looked after by my grandparents until I was two years old, then my father remarried and I went to live with him. All evidence of those early events was destroyed. I began finding out about all of this just before my stepmother died. I always wondered why I had such a hostile relationship with my father and why I could never really trust my stepmother.

I was cantankerous and was beaten for it, but could never really understand why. My long-suffering stepmother could not understand my father's peculiar behaviour, but eventually decided it was because I reminded him so much of his first wife. When I discovered my real mother, I tried to make contact with her. Sometimes she seems eager to know me, but at other times she wishes that I did not exist.

As a teenager I got into alcohol, drugs and child prostitution. I have now been off alcohol, drugs and out of the prostitution market for twenty-one years. I am currently in a monogamous relationship, surrounded by a number of caring people, and have a fulfilling job -- but still I do not feel right. Even though people tell me that "God has a plan," I say, "Yes, that is very nice, but you are not the one going through what I am going through." I constantly think about death and dying. I say, "Instead of being such a liability to society, if I died then nobody would really care." It is when I get despondent that things really hit hard, and I have often thought of killing myself.

People tell me that there are many good things about me -- that I am a wonderful artist -- but I cannot accept it. People see in me things that I just do not. I am told that my concern for unwanted animals, unwanted people, the pollution in our neighbourhood, unemployment, and particularly unborn babies, is a beautiful thing, but I cannot feel it. With some help I built a little chapel out of discarded limestone in our backyard. I have given a decent burial to hundreds of aborted babies near the chapel. Anybody who enters the chapel will tell me that they smell roses, but there are no roses in the area.

I am told that I am a very talented artist, but when I look at those pieces up in my attic, I do not believe that I did them. It is like somebody else did it. I like the work, but it is not 'me.' I have an inner feelings that I can hardly describe where I am just not worth anything. It has been with me ever since I can remember. I have spoken to a number of psychologists about this problem, but they do not really want to deal with it.

I know that I am a survivor, but I wonder why I am here in the first place. Is there any meaning to all of us? I know that God is there... I have no problems with that. But where I fit into the whole scheme of things after having gone through all of this escapes me. Sometimes I feel that the other half (my twin brother) who died is an awfully lot luckier than I am. I have a deep seated feeling inside me that I feel that I will never get over. Even death and dying do not bother me in the least. "Okay, if I go, I go. It is no big deal." When people get angry with me and say, "You will be sorely missed," I say "That is ridiculous. I am living on borrowed time as it is. I do the best with what I have got for the time I have been given. After that, I will be gone and no one will give a damn."

My mother was judge and jury for me and my brother. On two occasions I was sentence to die. For some particular reason I am a survivor. It is a mystery. I have survived two abortion attempts, many illnesses, child pornography, epilepsy, jaundice, drugs, alcohol abuse, child abuse, prostitution, cult activities and all of this ... for what!? I am incredibly insecure in my relationship and wonder how long it will last and how long I am going to last. I feel that everybody would be a lot better off if I died. I feel like I am a sponge on society and have been all my life.

I know that a death sentence was passed on me and still has to be carried out. That is why I always live on the edge. So, if it happens, who cares? I deserve to die. As far as suicide is concerned, well, at this point there is the old adage, "razor blades hurt, jumping off buildings makes you look rotten in front of the mortician, gas makes you sick, etc." But it is always an option if I get boxed into a corner emotionally. A couple of weeks ago it was really, really bad.

I did not realise how much anger there was, but I have a lot of anger toward my natural mom and a lot of unresolved anger against my father. I have tried all sorts of ways to resolve it and nothing happens. I know that people want me around, but it does not seem to make any difference. I am always making an excuse for my existence by helping other people.

I went to my dad and stepmother's gravesite. I said, "You know, you are *there* and I am *here*. I have survived all of that bull. I bury it with you. That is it, I am never coming back here again." Then I walked off. It was supposed to be a magic wand, but it was only a temporary help. I went back into the whole self-guilt trip again.

If I had an opportunity to talk to my mom I would say, "Why are you treating me the way you are? I have not been angry with you. Why, Mom, why?" I was hoping that she would be proud of me with all my artwork, but she said absolutely nothing. Maybe she cannot deal with the fact that she tried to abort me twice. She cannot accept herself and she cannot accept me as part of her. There is a lot I cannot figure out. If I cannot kill myself I guess I will have to keep trying to understand why.

Author's Note:
Jean Paul is a courageous, sensitive, loving artistic individual who is still struggling to work through the deep difficulties of his past. He thanks God that there are some loving people in his city who understand what he is going through and stand by him. He has become increasingly aware of how being an abortion survivor has affected his outlook and he wants to be able to deal with it. He feels the world should know what it is like to be an abortion survivor.

IMPLICATIONS FOR THE WORLD

With contraception and abortion much of society is attempting to gain a utopia based on the idea that "The first right of every child is to be wanted." Modern cant insists "every child must be a wanted child." However, if a person is not wanted, that person has no right to be. We have introduced a new existential fear into our world. Being alive now depends on being wanted. No one is safe any longer and all must struggle to stay wanted because not being wanted carries with it the death sentence. "My life or death depends on the fact that someone wants or doesn't want me. I have no intrinsic right to be. If I exist because I was wanted, I must fulfil the expectations that wanting person (parent or state) has for me. Somebody else always has a project for me." "My worth is not intrinsic, it depends on how much people want me and is therefore relative and extrinsic. If I have no absolute God-given worth, then no one else does. I am dispensable and so are they."

Research Results

We have been studying the effects of the Post-Abortion Survivor Syndrome. We used questionnaires to collect data from a number of countries. Our preliminary results indicate that, in our unselected sample of survivors, 27% felt their parents considered aborting them, 47% felt their chances of survival were diminished and 35% had aborted siblings. Being an abortion survivor affected their lives in many ways. 23% felt they did not deserve to be alive and 53% had difficulty knowing who they were.

Statistics

There are approximately 60 million abortions each year world wide. In some Eastern European countries 90% of women have had abortions, often seven or eight abortions per woman. In China, it appears that all pregnancies save one are terminated. Thus, in both areas a child's chance of surviving a pregnancy is 10-20%. Almost all children in these countries have at least one aborted sibling. In the United States approximately 70% of women have had an abortion by the time they are 45, and another 10-15% have contemplated having an abortion. If all these women had one child, about 85% of the children born in North America would be abortion survivors. Since some women who have had abortions never have any other children, it could be estimated that 75% of children born in western countries are abortion survivors.

Another way of calculating it would be to consider the fact that approximately one in three North American pregnancies end in abortion. In some cities, e.g. Washington, D.C., 50% of all pregnancies are terminated. Thus, within a particular family a child has a 50-70% chance of surviving. In addition, those children who are born after an abortion had been contemplated are also survivors.

In most western countries, abortion has been easily available since 1970. Thus, 80% of all 20-25 year olds are abortion survivors, or approximately one-quarter of the population. In Eastern European countries, abortion has been easily available since the 1920's, thus 80-90% of all people 70 years or younger are abortion survivors (which amounts to 75% of the population). In China, the "one child per family" policy was introduced in the 1980's. Therefore, 85% of children up to 10-15 years of age are abortion survivors. This would be approximately 10% of the Chinese population.

It seems reasonable to hypothesise that in any population with a large percentage being abortion survivors who have deep, unattended conflicts, there would be an impact on the overall functioning of that society. Is there any correlation between the percentage of abortion survivors in a country and the turmoil exhibited within that country? We need to determine ways of measuring and evaluating any relationship between the number of abortion survivors and the amount of political chaos, economic struggles and family disintegration. It seems that the Eastern European countries, with the largest numbers of abortion survivors, are most affected. We are also interested in determining whether there is a correlation between the number of abortion survivors and the amount of psychiatric morbidity expressed in terms of rates of hospitalisation and the size of medical costs in a country.

The Impact on Society - *Psychological Conflicts*

There is a series of interlocking mechanisms that arise from the conflicts generated by being an abortion survivor that are difficult to separate out. However, the following factors affect society and can be detected:

- *Mistrust*

As abortion survivors cannot trust their parents, they trust only themselves or each other. This makes it hard for anybody to negotiate contracts. Thus, people tend to resort to an array of lawyers and accountants and detailed contracts to support their side of a bargain. The other side must do the same.

50

- *Dishonesty*

Many abortion survivors have a deeply rooted tendency toward dishonesty. This is because, regarding some of the most critical issues within their family, they do not know what really happened and they are afraid to ask. They spend their young lives skirting around deeper truths. This tends to have a pervasive effect on their being able to look into many other aspects of themselves. Added to this is a dishonesty handed down by the parents. When the parents cannot admit to their deepest pain and most awful crime, it is difficult for them to be honest. Thus children collude with their parents and learn the same tendency to be evasive and deceitful.

- *Cynicism*

Because there was a major discrepancy between parents saying that they love their children while at the same time they had killed or contemplated killing one of them, abortion survivors tend to be cynical about many things. They doubt the sincerity of love, compassion, parental care and neighbourly concern. They are particularly cynical about directives from authority and tend to see good government directives as meaningless. The net effect of so many abortion survivors with these conflicts is that it is very difficult to conduct business with any speed. There is so much distrust, dishonesty, cynicism and disregard for authority that many business deals are made only with great scepticism and therefore batteries of lawyers and volumes of legal papers, all which tend to increase the cost of doing business and impede the speed of transactions.

- *Immaturity*

Many abortion survivors are afraid to mature. This is partly because they missed out on a secure, well-attached childhood, and partly because their future seems to uncertain. They do not want responsibility but complain about those who take it.

- *Lack of Gratitude*

Because abortion survivors are not sure they are happy to be alive, they are not easily satisfied and become easy targets for consumer producing media. Many tend to buy with very little purpose. With all their excess materials, they have to store their 'junk' in increasingly large 'u-store-it' sites.

- *Chronic Unhappiness*

Survivors tend not to experience joy and are often preoccupied with morbid concerns regarding their own lives. They are afraid to think about deeper things. To avoid unhappy feelings, they spend a good deal of time distracting themselves. This may be evidenced in their interest in violence and morbid sex in the media.

- **_Disregard for Authority_**

Abortion survivors tend to disregard all types of authority because they do not trust those into whose care they were born. Young people, who are angry about being held by the tenuous thread of 'wantedness', tend to be rebellious and wantonly destructive.

- **_Tenuous Relationships_**

Because they are unsure about their future, abortion survivors have difficulty making commitments. As a result, spousal support for pregnant women is less, and this (as indicated from our research) results in an increase in the chance of abortions and miscarriages.

Many abortion survivors are disinterested in having children. Thus, there is a decline in the population. A market economy cannot work, partly because there are fewer people to buy the goods produced, and partly because there are too few taxpayers to support the pension plans, old age securities, etc. of those who do much of the consuming.

- **_Re-enacting Tragic Triangles_**

Abortion survivors tend to be passive participants (or observers) who watch unhappy events unfold rather than attempt to correct them. This only adds to their feelings of guilt. Their various guilts are denied and seldom examined. This is especially true where current social philosophies teach that guilt is a bad feeling to be avoided at all cost and that it only occurs because simple-minded religious zealots hold to the outworn concept of sin.

- **_Increasing Abortions_**

Abortion survivors may feel anger toward their parents that they cannot deal with because they are afraid to lose a relationship that has always been tenuous. They may displace this anger onto their children. When this happens, they are more likely to abort, abuse or neglect their children.

- **_"Greenies"_**

Although abortion survivors have a concern for life, it is often expressed as a concern for the environment, rather than children. It is obvious that, unless families come first, preserving the environment has no specific direction or purpose.

- **_Hopelessness_**

With increasing abortion there are fewer children, and, consequently, a pervasive hopelessness for society. Hope is based on the need to preserve ourselves, our inventions and our environment for future generations. With fewer children there is less need to conserve. The hopelessness makes people less inclined to have children, and with diminishing children there is less hopefulness. Abortion survivors also have difficulty concerning themselves with the future of the world because their own future has been so uncertain.

- ***Disinterest in God***

Many abortion survivors are very sceptical about the existence of love since those who are supposed to have loved them most, and who often say they do, are the ones who have killed them. If their parents' love is expressed by terminating the life of an unborn sibling, they find it nearly impossible to believe that God the Father can be loving. Since there is such frequency in family breakdowns, it is unlikely that people have a good concept of what family relations are supposed to be. Often, when abortion survivors are told God the Father loves them they are so sceptical that they do not even bother to investigate whether He really does love them.

The overwhelming existential anxiety leads to the culture of death. Abortion survivors are reckless with their lives and the lives of others. "Life is cheap." They are fascinated with death. They fear being destroyed, yet are attracted to it. On the one hand, they feel, as most survivors do, that they are almost invincible (because they escaped a certain death once). Yet they continuously flirt with death. It is almost as if they needed constantly to dare death "to do it's work", to prove that they really are alive (this is seen in reckless driving, the taking of street drugs, promiscuous sex with the risk of AIDS, etc.). Abortion survivors are constantly playing Russian roulette with their lives and with the lives of others. Curiously enough, they also have a deep fear of death which for most signifies total annihilation. Not being able to project themselves in the future, they may have difficulties projecting themselves in eternal life. Given their desire to regress, death often means the return to a state of absolute non-existence, or the fusion with a mass, in which they loose all individuality. New Age type thinking and the Buddhist religion therefore exert a great attraction for abortion survivors.

TREATMENT

Prevention

To prevent the awful and frequent occurrence of surviving abortion there have to be fewer abortions. There are many routes to do this, but we suspect the best thing to do is increase the value and necessity of children. Abortion survivors have deep rooted conflicts which can only be resolved through a combination of psychotherapy, learning new behaviours, understanding environmental contingencies and transactions, and spiritual renewal.

Psychotherapy

Group psychotherapy[13] is both effective and efficient in achieving these ends. It should be followed by family therapy, which helps children deal with the secrets, gives parents some ideas of better ways to manage their children, and helps parents through the many confusions that have arisen because one or both are abortion survivors. The family then needs to become involved together in a project aimed at preventing the problems that brought them into difficulties. The ideal is intensive psychotherapy, but since there is so little of this available, counselling directed mainly at the existential guilt is very valuable, especially when individuals are supported by a church.

Spiritual Healing

Abortion survivors must be able to see that parental love is real. When they see it in people, they then can understand that God, as our Father, can be loving toward them. They need to understand that they are welcome in God's family, and that when they have God's Spirit within them He gives purpose, joy and meaning to their lives. Salvation through Jesus Christ is both the cause and effect in the healing process.

---

[13]   Ney, P.G. & Peeters, M.A. "Hope Alive", *Pioneer Publishing*: Victoria, Canada, 1996.

Conclusion

Abortion survivors are real people with serious conflicts that often result in social, psychiatric and medical problems. These arise from the fact that they have survived in a situation where their siblings or others have frequently died. There are at least ten ways in which they could be survivors, and these result in somewhat different symptoms. The core conflicts stem from their survivor guilt, their existential anxiety and their enormous distrust of themselves and others. They are not easy to treat, but hope and healing are available.

The behavioural manifestations may be of great importance, especially when it is possible that 80% of Eastern Europeans, 70% of North Americans and 85% of Chinese being born are abortion survivors. There may be a strong relationship between the social and economic difficulties in each of these areas and the number of abortion survivors.

A Stern Warning

It appears that we are heading for a human ecological disaster. Without an intervention by God to save us from the natural consequences of our own stupidity, it is quite likely that we will destroy the human race. This will be the natural consequence of disturbing a number of fine balances. It is only because of His grace that we have survived so well so far.

How does one prevent this from happening?

Repent

We have not been reacting hard and fast enough to pervasive problems. We are guilty of passivity. There are no innocent bystanders in matters of life and death, and there are millions of children dying from abortion and millions more becoming abortion survivors.

Warn

We must demonstrate to the world at large that this is a matter of grave concern to our human ecology. Speaking from an ecological point of view, it is better understood.

Value children

We must increase the value of children. When children are more valuable, people spend more time and effort in looking after them.

Healing the hurts

When the ones that have been most severely injured are healed, there is an exuberant expression of joy that is very convincing. If nobody else will stop the wholesale slaughter of unborn children, the survivors are those who can best speak of what happened.

Group counselling

There is an enormous need to heal these people, and it cannot be done individually. It can be done in groups, and we are now teaching group counselling in a number of centres.

Stop "wanting" children

Stop having children because you want them and stop telling them how much you wanted them.

Welcome

In the name of Jesus Christ, welcome every child, regardless of sex, size, intelligence, race or convenience.

Blessed are all those children who grow up in a home where abortion was not even considered. They are free from the very difficult conflicts surrounding abortion survivors. These children are not alive because they were wanted, but because they have an inherent right to life. Because they do not have to strive to stay wanted, they can be more independent and develop as God intended them to do. God-fearing physicians should have no fear of recognising the very unpalatable truth of abortion survivors. We hope that they will bring up the subject with their patients, especially when there are many psychosomatic symptoms for which there does not seem to be any other explanation. When they can broach the subject and explain Post-Abortion Survivor Syndrome to their patients, they will find there is often great relief. Later on, their patients may require extensive psychotherapy, but at least now they know why they have such an ambivalent attitude about life, their own in particular.

For God's sake, for the sake of all humanity, for your own and your family's sake, open your eyes and ears. See what underlies so much hopelessness in the world. It is millions of people who are not sure that they are glad to be alive when an innocent sibling died. Hear the chorus of reports depicting and predicting misery and chaos. It is likely to be the expression of people so deeply wounded that they do not care if they kill or are killed. Does it not occur to you that the chaos and confusion in this world is greatest where abortions and abortion survivors are most common? What is the connection? Having read this booklet, listen to your heart. Hear your inner perceptions of reality. If you can face your own most painful truths you will see reality. For then you will see that you may be contributing to the very dilemmas that you bemoan so loudly. Will the world experience yet another holocaust of pain and grief? It depends on your determination to know the truth of your own and your neighbour's suffering and/or destructiveness. Yes, you can know the truth and the truth will make you and all your neighbours free. But will you dare?

ABOUT THE AUTHORS

The authors come from different cultures and have different personal perspectives, but they have a similar view of the destructive way the world is treating children. Both authors have a deep desire to protect children by treating the roots of the problems that make them vulnerable scapegoats. They are now lecturing in a variety of countries and conducting training seminars in the treatment of Post-Abortion Syndrome, Child Abuse & Neglect and Post-Abortion Survivor Syndrome.

Marie Peeters is an American. After having obtained her medical training in Belgium and her paediatric speciality training in Canada, she worked in France with the world famous geneticist Jerome Lejeune and won an important scientific prize for her research in the biochemical causes of mental retardation. Her long association with *L'Arche*, where she worked with handicapped people, made her acutely aware of the danger of eugenics and the vulnerability of disabled people. She sees a desperate need for healing abortion and abuse trauma in Europe where, unless these are dealt with, the consequences will totally disrupt society. She is currently Director of Medical Research at the International Foundation for Genetic Research.

Philip Ney was raised in Canada, graduated in medicine from *The University of British Columbia* and trained as a child psychiatrist and child psychologist at *McGill University, University of London* and the *University of Illinois.* He has been an academic and a clinician for thirty years. He has taught in five medical schools, been full professor three times, served as academic department chairman, and established three child psychiatric units. He is currently Clinical Professor, Faculty of Medicine at the University of British Columbia. For many years he has done extensive research in child abuse and pregnancy loss and published more than twenty papers on the subject. In his early research he became aware of the connection between child abuse and abortion. More recently he has been studying children who are the survivors of abortion. He is presently conducting therapeutic groups for men and women who suffer from the effects of abuse and abortion. From that experience has come the book, *Ending the Cycle of Abuse* which has recently been published by Brunner/Mazel Publishers, New York.

ABOUT MOUNTJOY COLLEGE

Mount Joy College (MJC) is a growing nondenominational Christian registered college with high academic standards. Among other courses, MJC trains mature Christians from many places in the world to use Hope Alive group counseling to bring hope and healing to deeply damaged people. There are millions of people suffering the effects of unresolved pregnancy losses, particularly abortion, childhood mistreatment and being a survivor. MJC provides counselors training to understand the origin of basic conflicts, why tragedies repeat from one generation to another, how to resolve deep hurts and reconcile with those who hurt them and those whom they have hurt. .Since 1993 we have trained people to use Hope Alive in over 30 countries.

For more information,
dates of trainings and other courses:
www.mtjoycollege.com
&
www.messengers2.com
www.messengers2.org
www.messengers2.net

Resources from Mount Joy College
and Pioneer Publishing:

Deeply Damages (Third Edition), Philip G. Ney MD
* An explanation for the profound problem arising from infant abortion and child abuse
Ending the Cycle of Abuse: The Stories of Women Abused as Children and the Group Therapy Techniques that Helped Them Heal
* A book of personnel accounts from the experience of men and women in treatment, interwoven with a description of the treatment techniques that were used to help them resolve conflicts arising from early trauma........
The Centurion's Pathway (Second Edition) A Description of the Difficult Transition for Ex-Abortion Providers or Facilitators
* A description of how medical and para-medical personnel become the executioners of society's scapegoats. Personal testimonies show what made them change. It contains a clear guide for the painful pathway back to authentic humanity.
How to Talk to Your Children About Your Abortion
* Advice on sharing a difficult experience with children. It is an invaluable resource for parents who want to establish honest communications with their family.
The Law and Essence of Love. A Theoretical and practical treatise on all forms of authentic love.
Christian Principles for Palliative Care A thoroughly loving way to encourage and help people who are dying and those who support them.

and much more...
For more information or additional copies
Mount Joy College
P.O. Box 27103
Victoria, BC Canada V9B 5S4
Telephone: 250-642-1848, Fax: 250-642-1841
Email: mtjoycollege@islandnet.com
Pioneer Publishing
Victoria, BC Canada 1998

➤ Order form on www.messengers2.com